AMAZING FOOTBALL RECORDS

BY PAUL HOBLIN

Published by The Child's World®
1980 Lookout Drive • Mankato, MN 56003-1705
800-599-READ • www.childsworld.com

Acknowledgments
The Child's World®: Mary Berendes, Publishing Director
The Design Lab: Design and production
Amnet: Production
Red Line Editorial: Editorial direction

Design Elements: Mark Cinotti/Shutterstock Images

Photographs ©: Morry Gash/AP Images, Cover, 9, 21; Library
of Congress, 5; Scott Boehm/AP Images, 7; David Stluka/
AP Images, 11; Roberto Borea/AP Images, 13; Donna
McWilliam/AP Images, 15; Bill Kostroun/AP Images, 17;
Steve Broer/Shutterstock Images, 19; Daniel M. Silva/
Shutterstock Images, 23; AP Images, 25, 27, 29.

ISBN 9781614734031
LCCN 2012946498

Printed in the United States of America
Mankato, MN
November, 2012
PA02146

Disclaimer: The information in this book is current
through the 2011 NFL season.

ABOUT THE AUTHOR
Paul Hoblin has written several sports books. He has an MFA from the University of Minnesota. He plays many different sports.

TABLE OF CONTENTS

ONE

AMERICAN FOOTBALL

Football may seem like a funny name for the game. After all, the ball does not get kicked much. Players carry, pass, or catch the ball on most plays. Plus, in much of the world, the game of football is what people from the United States call soccer. In the late 1800s, athletes from the United States started to play a game that combined soccer and rugby. The result was American football.

There are some differences between American football back then and American football today. A touchdown used to be worth only four points. Now it is worth six. Another big difference is the equipment. Until the 1950s, there were no face masks or football helmets. Players back then were more likely to break their noses or chip their teeth.

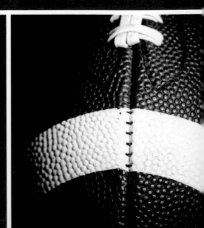

OLD-SCHOOL RECORD
In 1929, the Chicago Cardinals beat the Chicago Bears 40–6. Ernie Nevers scored all 40 of the Cardinals' points!

TOUGH *AND* GOOD

It is one thing to be tough. It is another thing to be good, too. Wide receiver Jerry Rice was both. He had at least one pass reception in 274  games from 1985 to 2004.

University of Syracuse and University of Carlisle football players play with little gear in a pre-1920s game.

A TOUGH QUARTERBACK

One thing all football players have in common is the need to be tough. Not many in the history of the National Football League (NFL) were as tough as Green Bay Packers quarterback Brett Favre. Like every football player, Favre had many injuries. He sprained joints, bruised muscles, and broke bones. But none of the injuries stopped him from starting the next game.

In 2003, Favre broke his right thumb. He threw with his right hand, so people thought he would have to stop playing. Favre did not agree. It was only the first quarter, so Favre went to the team doctor. The doctor made a **splint** for Favre's thumb. Then Favre returned to the game and threw two touchdown passes. He played the next game, too. And he played the next one and the one after that.

In fact, Favre kept playing games for seven more years. It was not until 2010 that he finally had to stop playing. He hurt his shoulder that year. The injury was so bad that he could not feel his hand. No one blamed him when he stood on the sidelines for the next game. After all, he had started 297 regular-season games in a row. That is the most consecutive games of any player in NFL history.

GOING FOR TWO

Most teams today kick the ball through the goal posts for an extra point after scoring a touchdown. But they have another option. They can "go for two." If they run or pass the ball into the end zone, they get two points instead of one.

Green Bay Packers quarterback Brett Favre drops back to pass the football during an NFL football game in 2003.

TWO

AMAZING FOOTBALL PLAYERS

Brett Favre was really tough, but he also was really good. His 297 consecutive games record is not his only record. He also holds the records for most touchdown passes, most passing attempts, most **completions,** and most passing yards.

FAVRE'S AMAZING CAREER

Favre's career had some amazing highs but also some lows. He holds many best and worst records.

BEST RECORDS		WORST RECORDS	
Most consecutive regular season games played by a player	297	Most intercepted passes	336
Most touchdown passes	508	Most fumbles	166
Most passing attempts	10,169	Most times being sacked	525
Most completions	6,300		
Most passing yards	71,838		

MOST PASSES

Favre may have thrown the most interceptions of all time, but that is only because he threw the most passes. Only 3.3 percent of those passes were intercepted.

Brett Favre (4) is pulled to the ground by Minnesota Vikings linebacker Ben Leber for a sack during a game in 2006.

THROWING A TOUCHDOWN ...
TO YOURSELF

As many touchdowns as Brett Favre threw, he never threw one to himself. In fact, only one player has ever done that. His name is Brad Johnson. In a game against the Carolina Panthers, the Minnesota Vikings quarterback tried to toss the ball into the end zone. Instead, his pass was **deflected** at the **line of scrimmage.** Luckily, the ball went right back to Johnson. He grabbed it out of the air and scrambled across the goal line. Johnson was given credit for both a touchdown pass and a touchdown catch.

MOST TOUCHDOWN CATCHES
1. **Jerry Rice: 197**
2. **Randy Moss*: 153**
3. **Terrell Owens: 153**
4. **Cris Carter: 130**
*Active as of 2012

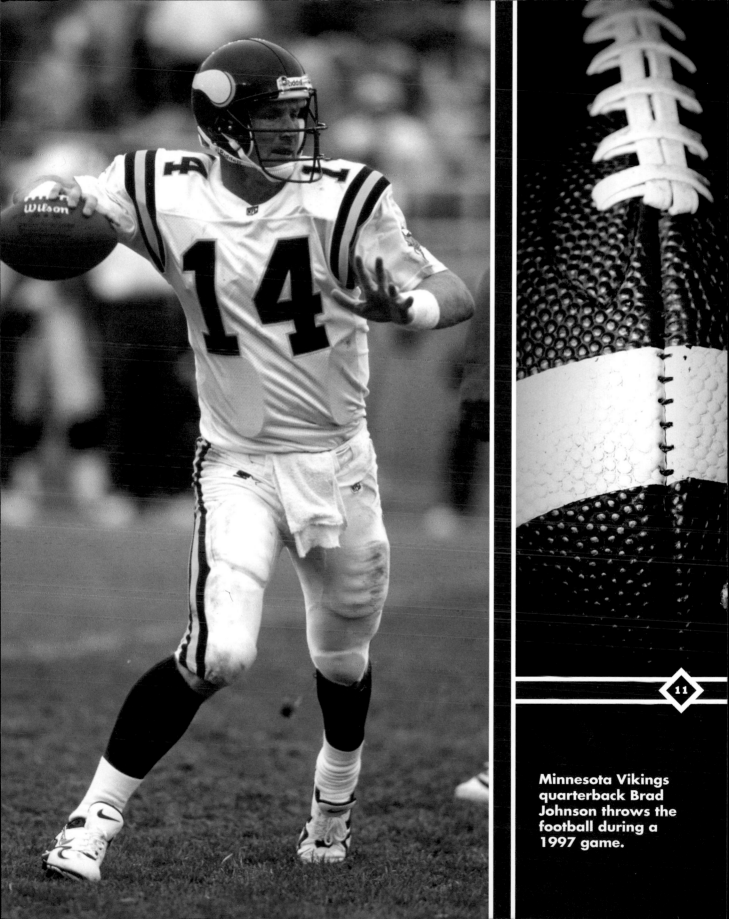

Minnesota Vikings
quarterback Brad
Johnson throws the
football during a
1997 game.

WHY PASS WHEN YOU CAN RUN?

Rushing is an important part of the game, too. Usually running backs do most of the running with the football. But the player who averaged the most yards each time he ran was not a running back. He was a quarterback. His name was Randall Cunningham. Quarterbacks usually spend most of their time throwing, but Cunningham was so fast that sometimes he ran instead. When he did, he usually gained a lot of yards. During his career, he averaged 6.36 yards (5.82 m) per carry. Another Eagles quarterback, Michael Vick, might break this record. He averaged 7.2 yards (6.6 m) per carry through 2011. If he keeps that up until his career ends, he will hold the record.

MULTI-TALENTED
After retiring as the NFL's all-time leading rusher, Emmitt Smith showed he was good at something other than running: dancing. In 2006, he won the *Dancing with the Stars* television competition.

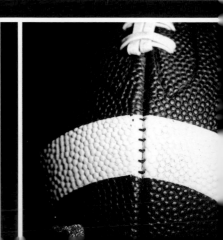

13

ALL-TIME LEADING RUSHERS (CAREER YARDS)

1. Emmitt Smith: 18,355 (16,783 m)
2. Walter Payton: 16,726 (15,294 m)
3. Barry Sanders: 15,269 (13,962 m)

Philadelphia Eagles quarterback Randall Cunningham heads toward the end zone in a game against the New York Giants in 1987.

BREAKING RECORDS IS EASY?

It isn't just **offensive** players who set records. **Defensive** players make and break records, too. One way defensive players stop offensive players from scoring is by sacking the quarterback. A sack is when a defensive player tackles a quarterback behind the line of scrimmage.

In the last game of the 2001 regular season, New York Giants' Michael Strahan needed just one sack to set the all-time single-season record for most sacks. But getting that final sack looked almost impossible for Strahan. The Green Bay Packers had a big lead with only a few minutes left to play. They would probably just hand the ball off to their running back until the end of the game.

ALL-TIME SACK LEADERS

SINGLE SEASON		CAREER	
Michael Strahan, 2001	22.5	Bruce Smith	200
Jared Allen, 2011	22.0	Reggie White	198
Mark Gastineau, 1984	22.0	Kevin Greene	160
Chris Doleman, 1989	21.0		
Reggie White, 1987	21.0		

Dallas Cowboys quarterback Anthony Wright (2) hits the ground after being sacked by New York Giants defensive end Michael Strahan in a 2000 game.

But the sack turned out to be easy. For some reason, Packers quarterback Brett Favre kept the ball instead of handing it off to his running back. Usually Strahan had to get past at least one lineman to reach the quarterback. But this time, no one tried to stop him. Suddenly, Strahan found himself looking straight at Brett Favre. Strahan did not even have to make a tackle. Favre fell down right in front of him. To get his record-breaking sack, Strahan simply had to touch the fallen quarterback.

Some people thought Favre fell on purpose to help Strahan get the record. But one thing is certain: Michael Strahan is now the all-time single-season leader in sacks.

A NEW STATISTIC

A sack did not become an official statistic until 1982. Of course, lots of great players were tackling the quarterback behind the line of scrimmage before then. So, we may not really know who holds the NFL sack records!

Brett Favre (4) pats defensive end Michael Strahan (92) after Strahan sacked him to set a new single-season sack record.

THREE

AMAZING FOOTBALL TEAMS

In the history of the NFL, there have been many really good teams. But only two teams have won every regular season game: the 1972 Miami Dolphins and the 2007 New England Patriots. In 1972, NFL teams played 14 games during the season. And the Dolphins had a perfect 14–0 record. They also won the Super Bowl that year.

BEST REGULAR-SEASON RECORDS (WINNING PERCENTAGE)

TEAM	RECORD	WINNING PERCENTAGE
2007 New England Patriots	16–0	100
1972 Miami Dolphins	14–0	100
1984 San Francisco 49ers	15–1	93.8
1985 Chicago Bears	15–1	93.8
1998 Minnesota Vikings	15–1	93.8
2004 Pittsburgh Steelers	15–1	93.8
2011 Green Bay Packers	15–1	93.8

WINNING COACH
Don Shula was the coach of the only undefeated team (regular season and playoffs) in NFL history: the 1972 Miami Dolphins.

The Patriots played against the Jets in an NFL playoff game in January 2007.

The 2007 Patriots had to play two extra games in the regular season. That meant they were the first team with a 16–0 record heading into the playoffs. They also won their first two playoff games. Like Miami, the Patriots had a chance to be undefeated in the regular season and win the Super Bowl. If that happened, many would consider them to be the greatest team of all time. Unfortunately, they could not quite do it. Their opponent, the New York Giants, barely beat the Patriots in the Super Bowl 17–14.

WORST RECORDS

Since 1970, there have been only two teams to have not won a game in a full regular season.

1. 2008 Detroit Lions: 0–16
2. 1976 Tampa Bay Buccaneers: 0–14

Detroit Lions quarterback Dan Orlovsky (6) reacts as he walks off the field after a 2008 NFL football game lost by the Lions.

RIVALS BECOME TEAMMATES

In the late 1930s and early 1940s, there was a rivalry between the Philadelphia Eagles and the Pittsburgh Steelers. Part of the reason for the rivalry was that both teams played in the state of Pennsylvania. Another reason was that neither of them was very good. In 1943, these rivals did something surprising: they became teammates. That year, many players from each team left to fight in World War II (1939–1945). So the owners decided to combine what was left of their rosters. For one full season, the Steelers and Eagles called themselves the Steagles. They did pretty well, too. They finished the season with a record of five wins, four losses, and one tie. It was the best year either team had ever had up to that point.

The Pittsburgh Steelers may not have been very good in the 1930s and 1940s. But ever since, they have been one of the NFL's best teams. In fact, they have more Super Bowl victories than any other team.

MOST SUPER BOWL WINS
1. **Pittsburgh Steelers: 6**
2. **San Francisco 49ers: 5**
   Dallas Cowboys: 5
4. **Green Bay Packers: 4**
   New York Giants: 4

FOOTBALL VETERANS
Several football players have fought in a war. They include all-time greats such as Roger Staubach and Otto Graham.

Steelers safety Troy Polamalu deflects the ball in the end zone in a 2008 game.

READY. . . BRRRREAK!

Like many sports, football is often played outside. Unlike baseball or tennis, though, the football season stretches into the winter. This means it can get really cold. Several NFL games have been played in 0°F (-17.8°C) weather.

The all-time coldest game was at Lambeau Field. On December 31, 1967, the Green Bay Packers beat the Dallas Cowboys 21–17 to win the NFL Championship. But the most memorable thing about the game wasn't the Packers' victory. It was the cold. At -13°F (-25°C), the players' toes and fingers and lungs were really cold. No one complained, though—not even the fans. The game was a sellout. "The fans were tough to stay out there and watch the game," one Cowboys player said. Ever since, this game has been called "The Ice Bowl."

COLDEST GAMES

GAME	DATE	TEMPERATURE
Dallas Cowboys at Green Bay Packers	December 31, 1967	-13°F (-25°C)
San Diego Chargers at Cincinnati Bengals	January 10, 1982	-9°F (-23°C)
Indianapolis Colts at Kansas City Chiefs	January 7, 1996	-6°F (-21°C)

BETTER THAN BLOWING INTO HANDS

During really cold games, the NFL uses heaters to help players stay warm on the sidelines. These heaters are designed to warm up the players' helmets and gloves, too.

After picking up the ball fumbled by Packers quarterback Bart Starr, Cowboys defensive end George Andrie (66) follows teammate Jethro Pugh (75) over the goal line to score in the December 31, 1967, NFL championship game.

FOUR

OTHER AMAZING FOOTBALL RECORDS

In 1934, the New York Giants played the Chicago Bears for the NFL Championship. The field was icy and both teams spent the first half slipping all over the place. Still, at halftime the Bears were able to take a 10–3 lead. That is when the New York Giants decided to change their shoes. Their cleats were not working on the ice. So they borrowed sneakers from a local college. The strategy worked. The Giants won the game 30–13.

ONLY ONE MISSED FIELD GOAL

In 1998, Gary Anderson was the first kicker to have a perfect season. He did not miss a single field goal or extra point all year. But in the National Football Conference championship game, Anderson finally missed. And his team, the Minnesota Vikings, lost in overtime to the Atlanta Falcons.

LONGEST CONSECUTIVE FIELD GOALS STREAK

SEASON	PLAYER	FIELD GOALS IN STREAK
2002–2004	Mike Vanderjagt	42
1997–1998	Gary Anderson	40
2005–2006	Matt Stover	36

SOCCER-STYLE

There are two ways to kick a field goal—with the front of the foot or with the side of the foot. Most NFL kickers are called "soccer-style kickers." It just means they use the side of their foot like soccer players do when kicking the ball.

Bronko Nagurski of the Chicago Bears is tackled by members of the New York Giants during the 1934 NFL Championship Game.

THE FOG BOWL

It was sunny in the first quarter of the Chicago Bears' 1988 NFC Playoff game against the Philadelphia Eagles. For the rest of the game, though, a cloud of fog rolled over the Chicago field hiding the sun and players. The fog was so thick that the announcers and fans often did not know what was happening on the field. Neither did the coaches. Players would run from the field to the sidelines to let the coaches know what had just happened. In the end, the Bears won the game 20–12.

104 YARDS, BUT NOT A TOUCHDOWN

In 2011, Percy Harvin caught a kickoff at the back of his end zone. He took off running. He ran across midfield, then the 40-yard line, then the 30, the 20, then the 10. Finally, with the opponents' end zone only 3 yards (2.7 m) away, he was tackled. Harvin had run 104 yards (95.1 m). That is the farthest any NFL player has ever run without scoring a touchdown.

LONGEST PLAYS IN NFL HISTORY

PLAYER AND YEAR	YARDS	TYPE OF PLAY
Antonio Cromartie, 2007	109 (99.7 m)	Missed field goal return
Randall Cobb, 2011	108 (98.8 m)	Kickoff return
Ellis Hobbs, 2007	108 (98.8 m)	Kickoff return
Devin Hester, 2006	108 (98.8 m)	Missed field goal return
Nathan Vasher, 2005	108 (98.8 m)	Missed field goal return

WASN'T THAT DANGEROUS?
Field goal posts used to be located at the front of the end zone. It wasn't until 1974 that they were moved to the back of the end zone.

A FIELD GOAL TO A KICK RETURN
If a field goal is kicked too short and missed, a player from the other team is allowed to catch the ball and run with it toward the opposite end zone.

Lights shine through the fog during the December 31, 1988, NFC Playoff game between the Chicago Bears and the Philadelphia Eagles.

GLOSSARY

completions (kuhm-PLEE-shunz): Completions are when a player throws the ball and a teammate catches it. Brett Favre holds the NFL record for most completions in a career.

consecutive (kuhn-SEK-yuh-tiv): Something that is consecutive happens one after the other. Johnny Unitas had at least one touchdown pass in each of 47 consecutive games.

defensive (di-FENS-iv): Someone on the defensive side of the team tries to stop the offense from scoring. Defensive player Michael Strahan set a record for sacks.

deflected (di-FLEKT-id): A deflected pass is blocked out of the air. Brad Johnson caught his own deflected pass.

end zone (END ZONE): The end zone is the area at the end of a football field where the ball must be carried or passed to score points. Percy Harvin caught a kickoff at the back of his end zone and returned it 104 yards.

line of scrimmage (LINE OV SKRIM-ij): The line of scrimmage is the imaginary line that separates teams at the beginning of a play. Brad Johnson's pass was deflected at the line of scrimmage.

offensive (uh-FEN-siv): Someone on the offensive side of the team tries to help his or her team score. Randall Cunningham was an offensive player for the Philadelphia Eagles.

sacked (SAKD): A sacked quarterback has been tackled by a defensive player behind the line of scrimmage. Brett Favre holds the record for being sacked.

splint (SPLINT): A splint is a piece of wood, plastic, or metal that offers support for a broken finger or limb. The doctor made a splint for Brett Favre's thumb.

LEARN MORE

Books

Berman, Len. *The Greatest Moments in Sports.* Naperville, IL:
Sourcebooks, 2009.

Jacobs, Greg. *The Everything Kids' Football Book.* Avon, MA:
Adams Media, 2010.

Weisman, Blaine. *Football.* New York:
Weigl, 2010.

Web Sites

Visit our Web site for links about football records:
childsworld.com/links

Note to Parents, Teachers, and Librarians:
We routinely verify our Web links to make sure they are safe and
active sites. So encourage your readers to check them out!

INDEX